Agnieszka and Włodek Bilińscy

Poland
The beauty
of architecture

almapress

Oficyna Wydawnicza Alma-Press, Warszawa

Lublin. Dominikańska Street.

Publisher's Note

Forests, meadows, rivers and fields are hiding the most beautiful jewels of our country's nature that wait to be discovered. The beauty of nature almost everywhere around us, not only in the renowned, generally accepted sanctuaries of nature, such as the Tatra Mountains or the Białowieska Forest. The previous album published by our house, "Picturesque Poland", showed a Poland different from the one you can see in tourist brochures or official promotional materials, as seen by two leading photographers, Agnieszka and Włodek Biliński. Out of hundreds of pictures taken all over the country at various times of the year, they have selected the best ones. But Poland does not mean just nature – it is also magnificent architecture, both well-known in the old cities that are every tourist's Mecca and forgotten, rarely admired, somewhere off the beaten track of all the tourist trails.

Agnieszka and Włodek Biliński manage to show both in a breathtaking way. The compositions and details being the focus of the photographs in the album "Poland. The bauty of architecture" really fill us with admiration and pride. The words of a poet spring to mind: "This is what Poland is like".

We have our personal favorites in this album, but we are not going to describe them, as even the best description would be useless. The album needs to be watched attentively and its atmosphere absorbed. The passage of time and beauty of architecture call for reflection. If we do read it in such a way, we could venture saying that both the authors and publisher have been successful.

We are certain that you will find the album ravishing. Perhaps it will make you see our homeland from a new perspective, so that you will be enchanted with its beauty, which was actually what the authors and publisher intended.

Warsaw. Underground station *Centrum* put to use in 1998 and the tallest (234 m) building in Pola – the Palace of Culture and Science, constructed in 1952-1955.

Warsaw. Castle Square and the Royal Castle, the seat of Mazovian princes, and since the beginning of the 17th c. — the residence of Polish kings. Completely destroyed during World War II, reconstructed in 1971-1988.

Old Town Market Square in **Warsaw.** It obtained its present form during the reconstruction in 1949-1963. In 1980 placed on the UNESCO World Heritage List.

Warsaw. Monument to Frederic Chopin.

Warsaw. A fragment of the Palace on the Water in the Łazienki Park, erected on the initiative of Stanisław August, the last Polish king, in the 2nd half of the 18th c.

arsaw. Palace in Wilanów, the suburban residence of King Jan III Sobieski, built in the 17th c.
iew from the courtyard.

arsaw. The garden facade of the Wilanów Palace.

Warsaw. Panorama of left-bank **Warsaw** taken from the opposite bank of the Vistula.

Cracow. A statue in the Waza Chapel at the Wawel.

Cracow. Panorama of the Wawel, the coronation site of 37 Polish kings.

racow. Sigismund's Chapel distinguished for golden dome — the most beautiful of the several chapels at the Wawel.

Cracow. Floriańska Street. In the background: the towers of St. Mary's Church in the Main Market Square.

Cracow. Cloth Hall – former 14th – century commercial stalls

acow. Towers of the Wawel Cathedral. The famous Sigismund Bell in the Sigismund Tower.

Gdańsk. Neptune's Fountain from 1633 – the symbol of the city which splendidly celebrated i▮ millennium in 1997.

Gdańsk. Piwna Street and St. Mary's Church, the largest church in Poland and one of the biggest Gothic churches in Europe.

Gdańsk. Old Town panorama with the Old Crane by the Motława.

Gdańsk. Długa Street in the Old Town at dusk. At the bottom of the street the Gothic Main City Hall with a 82-meter tower.

Szczecin. Pomeranian Princes' Castle reconstructed in 1945 in the Renaissance style to imitate appearance from the 16-17th c.

Szczecin. The city panorama from the opposite bank of the Odra river.

Szczecin. Wały Chrobrego – a representative street and Jana z Kolna Street.

Szczecin. Old Town Hall.

Szczecin. Apartment houses in the Old Market Square (Sienna Street).

czecin. St. Peter and Paul's Church (1470-1480).

Poznań. Old Market Square and the Renaissance Town Hall reconstructed in 1550-1555. Its ma
attraction is a pair of mechanical billy goats clashing horns at 12 noon sharp.

Poznań. The Baroque St. Magdalena and St. Stanisław's Parish Church constructed in 1651-1732.

Poznań. St. Peter and Paul's Cathedral in Ostrów Tumski. Mieszko I and Bolesław Chrobry, th first Polish king, are buried here. The first settlement was built here in the 9th c.

Wrocław. The Gothic Town Hall in the Old Town Market Square, built in 1327-1504.

Wrocław. In the Market Square.

Vrocław.
Ornaments at the top of the Mannerist apartment house called "Under the Griffins".

Vrocław. Apartment house facades on the eastern side of the Market Square.

Wrocław. Ostrów Tumski – an isle on the Odra river – the oldest part of the city.

Łódź. The second biggest city in Poland. The outlet of Piotrkowska Street onto Liberty Square.

Łódź. In the 2nd half of the 19th c. the world's biggest textile factories operated here. The former Greyer's factory.

Łódź. Former J.K. Poznański's plant.

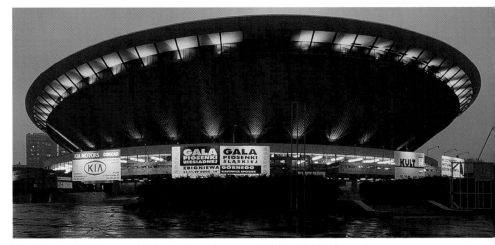

The biggest Polish arena in **Katowice** – the so-called "Spodek" (Saucer).

Katowice. Miners' housing estate – Nikiszowiec. Św. Anny Street.

Opole. City panorama from the castle tower in Ostrówek.

Opole. Apartment houses over the Młynówka Canal. The site of a Slavonic settlement already in the 8th c.

Opole. The Gothic Cathedral of the Invention of the Holy Cross from the 15th c. and a fragment the city walls.

zeszów. Town Hall

zeszów. The Lubomirski Castle. In 1939-1940 the Germans held the pre-war prime minister, 'incenty Witos, in the castle's prison.

Przemyśl. In the 18ᵗʰ c. it became the third biggest stronghold in Europe during the Austrian annexation. View from the Clock Tower.

Przemyśl. Royal Castle.

Lublin. In 1569 a union of Poland and Lithuania was concluded here. Jezuicka Street.

Lublin. A fragment of an apartment house facade the Market Square.

Lublin. View on Krakowskie Przedmieście Stre and the New Town Hall.

Lublin. Apartment houses in the Castle Square.

Lublin. View from the
Grodzka Gate on the
Royal Castle.

Zamość. This "Padua of the North" was founded in 1580 by Chancellor Jan Zamoyski. Today it the best preserved Renaissance town in Poland. View on the Town Hall from Grodzka Street.

Zamość. Apartment houses in the Great Market Square.

Zamość. Apartment house arcades in the Italian style.

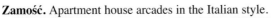

Toruń. Beside Cracow, the most pr cious historical architectural comple in Poland. Monument to Nicola Copernicus, born in Toruń.

Toruń. Fragment of the mediev Town Hall and Artus Court.

Toruń. Slanting Tower.

Bydgoszcz. Stary Fort Street on the Brda river.

Bydgoszcz. Modern buildings on the Brda river.

Płock – the historical capital of the Mazovia, the actual capital of Poland in the 12th c. The classicistic Town Hall.

Kalisz. The oldest written account about the city (Calisia) dates from the 2nd c. Basilica Minor.

Gniezno. The coronation site of the first five Polish kings. The Cathedral. The Gniezno Doors leading to it are considered the masterpiece of Polish Romanesque art.

Gniezno. In the Market Square.

Zielona Góra. A city founded in the 16th c. Th[e]
Town Hall.

Zielona Góra. The Old Market Square.

Jelenia Góra. After obtaining municipal rights in the 12ᵗʰ c., it successively belonged to the Piasts, Bohemia and the Habsburg monarchy of Prussia and Poland. The Town Hall.

Jelenia Góra. Apartment houses in the Market Square.

Stargard Szczeciński. One thousand years ago Slavonic burg on the Ina. St. Mary's Church.

Stargard Szczeciński. The biggest in West Pomerania and richly decorated Town Hall and the Odwach Museum.

Kołobrzeg. A Slavonic settlement was founded here already in the 7th c. The Collegiate Church of the Immaculate Conception of the Holy Virgin Mary.

Frombork. Nicolaus Copernicus lived and worked here. It is here he wrote *On the Revolutions of the Heavenly Spheres*. The cathedral church. Copernicus' burial place.

Sandomierz. One of the most beautiful Polish towns towers on the slope by the Vistula. It has an extraordinary network of underground streets. The Town Hall.

Sandomierz. The Cathedral of the Birth of the Holy Virgin Mary.

Sandomierz. Old Town roofs.

In the market square of **Sandomierz**.

Kazimierz Dolny. A magical and unique place, where nature and architecture are delightfully harmonized, a charming location among loess hills intersected with ravines. The city panorama from the Three Crosses' Mount.

Kazimierz Dolny. The market square at dusk.

stochowa. The religious capital of Poland, besieged in vain by the Swedish and other armies ng the "flood" in 1655. The Sanctuary in Jasna Góra. It houses the painting of God's Mother of stochowa, an object of religious cult.

Książ Castle. On the edge of a steep promontory surrounded by the deep valley of the Pełcznica raises one of the most beautiful castles in Poland. It was constructed in the 13th c. upon the initiative of Bolek I, the prince of Świdnica, at the site of an older burg, later rebuilt and developed in the Baroque style among others. It was given its present, fabulously eclectic form in the early 20th c.

Czocha Castle in Lower Silesia. Its mysterious history goes back to the 14th c. It intertwines with the history of the Polish, Czech and German borderland. It belonged to the Łużyce lineage of the Uchtritz. It owes its present form to Ernest Gutschow, the castle's owner until the end of World War II.

Rzucewo. Neo-Gothic palace from 1845.

Nidzica. The Gothic Teutonic Knights' castle.

The early Baroque Lubomirski Palace in **Łańcut**. Magnificent magnates' residence with a unique collection of vehicles and horse-drawn carts.

Niedzica. A castle situated on a rocky hill, 20 m above the surface of the Czorsztyn Reservoir.

Tyniec. A complex of the Benedictine abbey, picturesquely located on a steep calcareous rock the Vistula.

Malbork. A huge stronghold towers over the Nogat, once the property of the Teutonic Knight Order, the Great Master's seat. In the middle ages it was among the greatest defense construction practically unconquerable, the world's largest brick castle, surrounded by strings of defense wal with towers and gates.

ozłówka. Zamoyski Palace Complex. The palace was built for the Bieliński family in mid-18th c. in the late Baroque style. The residence obtained its present shape over one hundred years ago, thanks to the efforts of Count Konstanty Zamoyski.

ieborów. The palace near Łowicz was acquired by the Radziwiłł family in the second half of the 8th c. Helena and Hieronim Radziwiłł made it their residence, adjoining the fantastic garden, rcadia.

We recommend you also miniatures of album „Picturesque Poland" in three languages

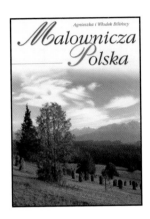  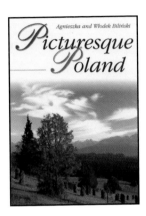

We invite you as well to familirize with our other albums about Poland

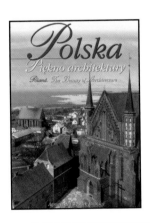 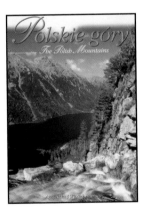 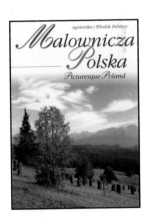

❐ Editor: *Jacek Zyśk* ❐ Layout: *Włodzimierz Kukawski*
❐ Translation: *Witold Biliński, www.fotobank.babel.pl*
❐ Cover design: *Foqs* ❐ Prepress Studio Wydawniczo-Graficzne DualArt Sp. z o.o.
❐ Printing house: *P.U.P. ARSPOL,* Bydgoszcz, I ed. Warszawa 2003 ❐ ISBN 83-7020-300-0
Copyright © Alma-Press Warszawa 2003
❐ Oficyna Wydawnicza „Alma-Press" ul. Lędzka 44a, 01-446 Warszawa, phone: (0-22) 837-10-84,
almapress@Qdnet.pl, http://**www.almapress.com.pl**